Y0-BVQ-050

WORDS ABOUT BIRDS
in
RHYME TIME
by
Eugene McAllister

© 1984 by The Olive Press Publications. All rights reserved.
Printed in the United States of America.

ISBN 0-933380-27-5

No part of this book may be reproduced in any form or by any
means without the written permission from the publisher.

First printing 1984

The Olive Press Publications
Jim Norris
P. O. Box 99
Los Olivos, California 93441

Cover photo by Bruce Fall

Cover design and book layout by Morgann Tayllor Jack

"I can say honestly that I find your bird verses delightful... your verses scan; your observations are Nashy without being gnashy."

- Los Angeles Times columnist Jack Smith -

A letter to Gene McAllister in January 1974

"The truly original pieces of literature come in small, valuable packages of philosophy and imagination in which their authors have revealed something new from the hidden recesses of the mind. Eugene J. McAllister, 'Poet Unlimited', was one of these valuable persons who wrote valuable ideas."

- Lompoc writer Robert Morris -

April 25, 1981

"Our Record poet, Eugene McAllister, came in last Friday with a poem he wrote while we were relieving the society editor on vacation. He said he 'chickened out' about giving me the poem at the time, but now it can be told:

I stopped at her desk to see Betty Laurent;
Found Editor Crompe instead.
I grinned, he scowled, away I went
Leaving all thoughts unsaid."

- Lompoc Record editor Harry Crompe -

August 21, 1968

In June 1977, Mr. Crompe in his Thoughts While Shaving column lauded Gene McAllister's "wonderful poems... Gene provided many incisive thoughts to this page, not to mention the many chuckles. An extremely talented fellow..."

Confession

To those of you who read by trash
And find that our opinions clash,
Don't take me seriously; At times
I say it just because it rhymes.

- Eugene McAllister -
Lompoc Record - March 9, 1970

Gene McAllister was a gentle man. But his wit was keen. It sliced through the pompous, the hypocritical, the foolish. He made us laugh at ourselves, re-examine our values, and occasionally get angry. His poems were all the more powerful because of their brevity.

Over 1500 of McAllister's verses were published, most of them from 1965 to 1977 in the Lompoc Record. He was also published in Look Magazine, the Los Angeles Times, Wall-Street Journal, American Legion Magazine and The California Herald.

A nature lover, Gene was fond of birds. In 1974, he selected 35 of his bird poems for book publication and asked me to illustrate them with line drawings. (I was then known as Wilma Jack). The search for a publisher was shelved, however, after Gene became ill.

This is the posthumous realization of his dream, under the auspices of the Lompoc Museum, to which he donated his large collection of prehistoric artifacts.

Gene McAllister is gone, but his words live on.

We will not see his like again.

- Morgann Tayllor Jack -

May 19, 1984

iv

Eugene McAllister was born February 22, 1900 - George Washington's birthday. As a small boy, he thought all the flags flying that day were hoisted just for him.

Later he served under the flag. He joined the U.S. Marine Corps in World War I and served as Red Cross field director in World War II. He was only 18 when he was accidentally shot while on Military Police duty in France. His right arm was permanently disabled.

But it didn't keep him from finishing high school upon his return to this country, from playing football, from teaching, or from writing.

Born in Pawnee City, Nebraska, Gene taught for three years at Ventura Junior College and then moved to Monrovia High School where he spent 28 years. He taught physical education and coached basketball, football and track. In later years, he was coordinator for audio-visual activities.

Photo by Suzanne Schwark

Gene McAllister and his wife Dorothy at their 50th wedding anniversary celebration June 20, 1975.

He and his wife Dorothy moved to Lompoc in 1964 after his retirement from the classroom. But Gene didn't retire from life. Between writing verse for publications, he and Dorothy enjoyed camping trips together. He was also adept at finding and cataloguing prehistoric artifacts. His collection is now on permanent display at the Lompoc Museum.

Some years before he died, Gene made:

ONE LAST REQUEST

Don't lay my body in a grave,
Don't put my ashes in an urn.
Scatter them upon the wave;
When I depart, I won't return.
Death, for man, is his release.
It frees a soul to go in peace.

And so it came to pass.

Eugene McAllister died April 25, 1981, in Lompoc after a lengthy illness, and was buried at sea in the Santa Barbara Channel.

Dorothy, his wife of 55 years and their daughter, Jane Shelton, still reside in Lompoc, along with two grandchildren and two great-grandchildren.

CONTENTS

DEDICATION   iii

REMEMBRANCE   v

POEMS

ACKNOWLEDGEMENTS

WORDS ABOUT BIRDS
in
RHYME TIME
by
Eugene McAllister

Illustrations by Wilma Jack

THAT'S THE WAY THE WIND BLOWS

Perhaps you've heard of the Lompoc bird.
In a week of wacky weather,
If he leaves a shelter he's blown helter-skelter
And left without a feather.

BIRDS I VIEW

Building a house for a finch is
    a cinch
But hear this before you begin it:
I looked in a house I had built for
    a finch
And in it discovered a linnet.

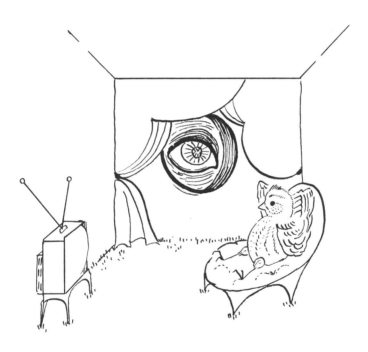

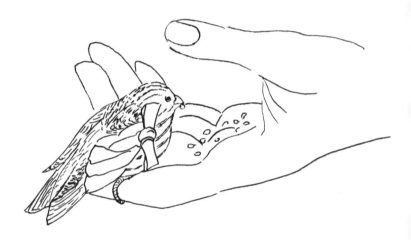

A WORD ABOUT A BIRD

To get involved with helpless birds, I've always been a cinch
And now I'm birdy-sitting with an injured lady finch.
First, extremely apprehensive, I am glad I acquiesced;
She has been so entertaining as a convalescent guest.

When we met she scolded loudly, pinched a finger in her beak,
But adjusted to confinement as a wing was very weak.
Dandelion buds, wild bird seed, Quaker oats and apple cores
Are the staples in her diet and the foods that she adores.

It has been three weeks. She's airborne and free to fly away
But, with a purple partner, she returns throughout the day.
If they raise a family, I hope she'll teach her tweets
To keep their eyes on motor cars when flying over streets.

POLITICAL BIRDS OF THE AIRWAVES

There is little of merit
In birds like the parrot
So continuously chorusing
 "foul."
There is partisan talk
From the dove and the hawk
So, for wisdom, we'll stay
 with the owl.

BIRD TABLE

There's a most unhappy sparrow perched upon my garden wall.
He hasn't had his breakfast; the blackbirds ate it all.
I have counted four and twenty, reminiscent of the rhyme,
They always eat his breakfast when he isn't here on time.
At the moment I am tempted, an old recipe to try;
That special one that calls for four and twenty in a pie.

THE ROADRUNNER

I wonder, when I see him run
Across the desert in the sun,
If he doesn't sometimes yearn
To be a cool young arctic tern.

SEA BIRDS CONFER

When our flower fields lie fallow, enjoying winter lulls,
They furnish pleasant refuge for a meeting of the gulls.

NOTHING NEW

The peacock likes to roost in trees
On branches swaying in the breeze.
The swan, with wing protecting head,
Sleeps soundly on his waterbed.

WILDLIFE NOTES

The mudhen's proper name is coot
And we agree that she is cute.
Of course no sportsman ever shoots
At coots.

DISTURBING THE BALANCE

Feeding wild birds, one of those fashionable trends
That adds to a list of one's fine-feathered friends,
Is gaining in favor and no one pretends
To know, ecologically, what it portends.
Suppose pampered birds become docile and fat
And such easy prey for some neighborhood cat,
That he loses all interest in gopher and rat.
Nature forbid it should all come to that!

NO CHICKEN DELINQUENTS

A mother hen is strict with her chicks.
She checks on everything checkable.
She promptly pecks all errant chicks
'Till each of her brood is impeccable.

OF BELLS AND BIRD SONGS

While I profess my admiration
For a tintinnabulation,
I must confess my fancy favors
Hemidemisemiquavers.

CUSTOMER CONVENIENCE

This has been my observation
At a wild bird feeding station
Where tubes of sugar water are
    supplied;
Hummingbirds are built to use
    them;
In-flight-refuelling won't
    confuse them
But it handicapped the others
    when they tried.
Now, convenient little perches
Put an end to frantic lurches
As a warbler, finch, and white-
    crown sip with pride.

GULL WATCHING

We watch a flight of gulls as
    they pass by;
Admire perfection in the way
    they fly.
The scene, a rare enchantment
    lends;
These are Jonathan Livingston's
    friends.

NATURE'S WAY

We should say a kind word for a much maligned bird
Often thought of as lacking in culture.
He removes roadside beasts that have long been deceased
And, for this, we owe much to the vulture.

BASIC TRAINING

I must tell you a story with merit:
A sailor came home with a parrot.
    It remembered each word
    It shouldn't have heard
And always was anxious to share it.

BIRD WATCHER'S REPORT

The bird bath ablutions of visiting blackbirds
Cause resident sparrows concern.
The fact of the matter, they splatter the latter
When they are awaiting their turn.

THE DROPOUT

One wild goose from a flock on the loose
Remained at a farmer's pond.
He became a recluse and was labelled obtuse
Because he refused to respond.

PREJUDICIAL CONDUCT

You would never guess if you didn't
    know;
Magpies are relatives of the crow.
Their black and white plumage makes
    them charmers,
But not, of course, to all those
    farmers
Who tell us that the crafty felons
Rob them of their fruits and melons.

A BIRD'S EYE VIEW

People point at us and whisper.
We never hear them shout.
This gives us the impression
We are being talked about.

WET FEATHER WEATHER AT THE ZOO

The parrot cage is situated
Where the rain falls unabated.
There is simply no way,
On a rainy day,
To keep Polly unsaturated.

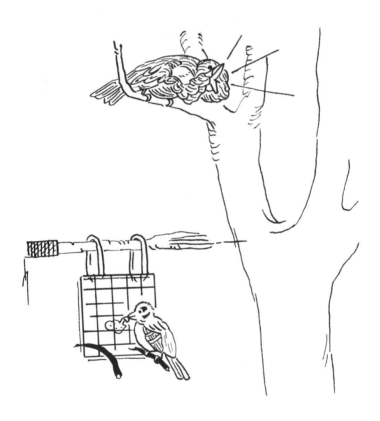

REDWINGED BLACKBIRD

That bird in the tree has been
    scolding me
For perhaps an hour or more.
We breakfast together in all
    kinds of weather
On opposite sides of the door.
The money I've spent just to
    keep him content
Seems wasted when he's in this
    mood,
And at times I despair and I
    solemnly swear
He will get no more of my food.
He is raucous and bold and he
    just loves to scold,
He is arrogant, selfish and narrow
But I hope he will stay for I'm
    happy to say
Every day he is bluffed by a
    sparrow.

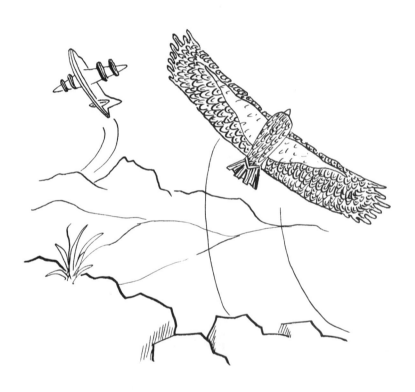

A VANISHING SPECIES

Airmen share the "wild blue yonder"
With the California condor.
They organize their flights
In deference to the condor's rights.

FASHION NOTE

Most male birds are fancy; the mates are rather plain.
Nature has good reasons, ornithologists explain.
Couples wearing look-alikes, listen to these words:
Your clothing is attractive but it isn't for the birds.

ON SUNDAY MORNING

Pigeons perch upon a church
For billing and for cooing;
Making nervous those in service
Could be a flock's undoing.

REMOVING ALL DOUBT

The early bird catches the worm.
If you are one of the latter,
The earliest bird will confirm
That you, to him, really matter.

BIRD BEHAVIOR

Birds of a feather flocking together
Are not necessarily friends.
The presence of food may trigger a feud
And that is when friendship ends.
Some of them fight over each little bite
And keep up a constant fuss;
In fact they're so rude that we must conclude
They have learned their bad habits from us.

NEVERMORE

I asked a raven I happen to know,
"Have you ever heard of the poet Poe?"
"Sir," said he, "Upon my oath,
Great Grandpa was the one who quoth."

BIRD WATCHING

Bird books, binoculars, soft-whispered words.
These are the watchwords of watchers of birds.
Their eyes scan a meadow, a marsh, a church steeple
And while they are watching, the birds watch the people.

SMORGASBIRD

A whitecrown feeds on wild bird seeds,
A song sparrow takes a bath,
A warbler steals the hummer's meals;
A hummer shows his wrath.
The finches flee the peanut tree
When blackbirds come to call.
Through window pane, in sun and rain,
We now enjoy them all.

SMORGASBIRD

NERVOUS BIRDS

Viewed ecologically, essentially
All birds must feel
They are logically, potentially
Somebody's meal.

TURKEY TALK

The future for a turkey is murky.
If you were he, you'd agree.

BACKLASH

The birds give me greetings with twitters and tweetings
Up there in a towering pine.
There's a pause in my fishing while I stand there wishing
That I could recover my line.

HE WENT THATAWAY

The hummer, as perhaps you've heard,
Has always been a busy bird;
A now-you-see-him-now-you-don't,
So look up quickly or you won't.

VANDENBERG BLACKBIRD

To show the importance he attaches
To uniforms worn at the Base,
A Vandenberg blackbird wears shoulder patches
And flies with easy grace.

Number _736_ of 1500

ACKNOWLEDGEMENTS

We wish to thank the many people who, through their caring and enthusiasm, have made the publication of this book possible.

Along with those already acknowledged within these pages, special thanks go to Mrs. Eugene McAllister for the permission to use additional poems and biographical material; to the Lompoc High School Graphic Arts class and instructor John Bullock for donating the typesetting done by Sheila Tompkins; to Rick Storms, president of the Lompoc Museum Associates Board of Trustees; Lucille Christie, Lompoc Museum director; Jim Norris of The Olive Press Publications; and the Lompoc Valley News.